Mothers

of the Upper Country

*A compilation of thoughts
on mothers and motherhood*

By

Carol Cutler Bumgarner
Marie DeKnikker
Bonnie Evans
Cindy Loggins Hale
Heidi Hoskins
Sandra Lund
Jennifer Neider

Keithley Creek Publishing, LLC
2275 Keithley Creek Road
Midvale, ID 83645
keithleycreek@gmail.com

Mothers of the Upper Country 2018

ISBN: 978-1-7322412-0-6

Need more copies? This title is available on Amazon.com.

For a mother like no other

Contents

Fields of Gold

By Carol Cutler Bumgarner

Whenever I go "below" as the lower country is referred to, I can't wait to head back up north, and top the Midvale Hill. The very sight of Hitt and Cuddy Mountains, the beautiful valleys and the Weiser River has always brought, and continues to bring, such peace to my soul.

The following story is a glimpse into my life as a farm-wife, business owner, and most importantly, a mother in the small town of Cambridge, Idaho. The story begins over sixty years ago in the nineteen-fifties. I call them the "golden years" of the Midvale-Cambridge area.

In those days, everyone knew everyone, and almost everyone was related in one way or another. When you came over the Midvale Hill, you entered a world starkly different from the one you had left "down below." It seemed as though time had stood still about fifty years earlier. The colorful characters who lived here at that time were right out of Mayberry, R.F.D.

There was no law enforcement as such up here. We rarely needed it. There was virtually no crime. People

would go on trips, be gone for days, or weeks, and leave their homes unlocked. We could park our cars on the main street with the keys in it, and a purse on the seat. It could sit there all night, and no one touched it. Keep in mind the Upper Country hadn't been discovered yet.

We knew every child, and who the parents were. Each child was treated as if it were your own. If he or she needed a hug, and the parents weren't there, you gave them a hug. If a child needed a scolding, or smack on the behind, you gave them that, too. Then you called the parents, and told them why, and they thanked you for it. If a child got into trouble at school, he was in trouble when he got home. Back then, kids were taught to respect authority. That may have had a lot to do with the low crime rate in the area. Cambridge was a place where you didn't worry too much about your kids getting into trouble, because someone was always watching, and the kids knew that any misdeeds would be known to their parents before the kid ever got home. It sure was a great time and place to raise kids!

Until I was fifteen years old, I was raised in the mountains of Idaho. My family was a timber family, and most of my time was spent in the woods. My heart belonged to the mountains, but when in the summer of nineteen fifty-five, I moved with my family to the small town of Cambridge, and fell in love with a local

farm boy, my heart turned to him, the land and the Upper Country.

We were married in the fall of fifty-six.

I could tell you just about anything you wanted to know about the lumber business, but I didn't know beans about farming. I would soon find out what it meant to be a farm-wife.

One day shortly into my marriage, I answered a knock on my door to find my mother-in-law standing there. "You are cooking for the hired men from now on," she said, without a greeting or an explanation. She just turned on her heel and walked away.

I was just seventeen years old, and that became my job for the next forty years, among many others.

Next, my husband decided it was time to teach me to drive the tractor. My first job was to drive the tractor while, he and a neighbor got some bales ready to take from the field.

They attached what they called a slip to the back of the tractor. The slip consisted of a couple of two-by-twelve boards about eight feet long, with a three-inch gap between the two boards.

The men would stack eight bales, two tiers high on the slip, with the tractor moving, insert a large crowbar into the ground between the boards, and the bales

would slide off in a neat little pile. One man would run alongside the slip and load the bales, while the other man stood on the slip and pushed the stack off with the crowbar.

So, I climbed onto the tractor, and Jim showed me how to shift gears. I put it into low gear, as instructed, and began driving slowly along the rows of bales while the two guys did their respective jobs behind the tractor.

But being the take-charge girl that I was, I decided that I'd better speed up or this job would take all day. Using my newly-acquired skills at tractor driving, I shifted into a higher gear and sped up. I was sailing along nicely, and proudly turned to give them a self-satisfied smile.

To my everlasting humiliation, I saw bales of hay scattered every which way, and the two men running after me to slow me down. Tractor lesson number one: *Faster is not always better!*

A few years later, when I had gotten so I could maneuver a tractor in the field pretty well, Jim wanted me to take the tractor with a harrow hooked on behind, from the barnyard to a field in the upper end of the ranch.

I had never driven the tractor outside of the field before, and I was a little nervous about it because I would have to come out onto Highway 71, and in a few

hundred feet, turn again onto Rush Creek Road, and cross the old, narrow bridge. About a half-mile further, I had to negotiate a sharp angled turn, and cross an old sunken culvert over the barrow pit.

I was told that after crossing the ditch, I was to turn into the field, follow the fence-line far enough ahead to clear the gate and leave room for Jim and his dad who were following behind me with other equipment.

I had worried about all the twists and turns, especially getting across that narrow culvert without dropping a wheel into the ditch.

I had started out cautiously, overcome all of the obstacles, and was finally turning into the field. Yea! I was so relieved as I started up the fence-line and got far enough forward to where I thought I could stop.

I looked back to check on my position, and to my horror I saw Jim jumping up and down, wildly waving his arms, and shouting things I'm glad I couldn't hear. My father was laughing so hard he couldn't catch his breath.

Then I could see that the harrow hadn't quite cleared the gate. It had hooked a post and taken out several sections of fence: posts, wires and all.

When I shut the tractor down, Jim didn't say a word to me. His dad was still laughing. He knew that Jim was

going to have to rebuild all of that fencing. I thought that maybe it was payback for some past transgression on Jim's part, when he was learning to drive a tractor. Tractor lesson number two: *Always watch your rear end.*

One thing I didn't do on the ranch was milk the cows. Jim tried to teach me, but I wasn't any good at it, and he finally gave up. We had twenty-two milk cows at that time, and all of the milking was done by hand.

Through the years I chuckled every time I remembered my mother's advice on my wedding night.

I was such a young, naïve bride, and I'd always heard that a mother's advice should be sought by a girl before her wedding. So I asked her if there was something she thought I should know. She looked me square in the eye, and very seriously she said "Whatever you do, don't learn to milk those cows, or you will be responsible for them for the rest of your life."

I learned to walk for miles fixing fences. I had my own horses, and I learned to round up cattle, to herd cattle, vaccinate, doctor and feed cattle. I learned to set irrigation dams for crops, to bale hay, to plow and harrow the fields.

I learned to plant, to grow, weed, harvest and can a large garden, and then cook it all for a crew of farm hands and a bunch of kids.

I learned to cut, perm and style hair. I learned how to landscape the yard, trim the trees, and mow the lawn.

I learned to clean fish and all kinds of wild birds. I learned to cook wild game so it tasted good. I learned where all the wild apples and berries on the ranch were located, and I learned how to turn them into delicious jams, jellies, apple butter, apple sauce and pies for my family.

I learned to do this, and so much more, all the while herding four little kids around, caring for their needs, and loving every minute of it.

But as hard as I tried, I could never learn to milk those cows! Thanks, Mom! That was the best advice I ever got.

One other precious gem of knowledge my mother shared with me on that long-ago night was to keep from having too many babies, too fast. She told me to sleep with my feet in a fruit-jar. I didn't figure that one out until many years later, and it was too late! I gave birth to three babies in two-and-a-half years, and a fourth one two years later. They were all under the age of five years. My mother, the comedian. Thanks, Mom. They have been the joy of my life.

Those four wonderful kids worked alongside their dad and me from the time they were barely big enough to walk. I am so grateful for them, and I'm very proud to

be their mother. We could never have accomplished all that we had to do without their cooperation and willingness to help. It took a team effort on everyone's part just to get through a day.

In 1970, we purchased Bucky's Café in Cambridge, and for the next fifteen years we were simultaneously running two full-time businesses.

During these years the girls, ages eleven and twelve, were working with me in the restaurant. They cleaned the tables, did the dishes, and helped the cooks. This was the same kind of work they had helping me with on the ranch since they were seven or eight years old. They started pouring coffee for the customers at the counter, and by the time they were fourteen years old they could wait tables with the best of them.

They got paychecks that went into a savings account. They made good tips that they could spend as they wished. Those two girls bought a good share of their own clothes, and all of their makeup and other frills. They had enough money in their savings to buy their own cars by the time they graduated high school. The two boys, ages eight and thirteen, worked with their dad on the farm, and also earned money according to their individual abilities. By the time they were fifteen years old, there wasn't a piece of farm equipment that they couldn't operate.

For years it seemed that most of my time was spent working. I'd leave the ranch to work at the café, then leave the café to work at the ranch. Most of my work days were eighteen to twenty hours long. I had been blessed with good health and stamina, not to mention an incredible tenacity.

The fortunate thing was that we could keep our kids with us while we worked. It gave us the opportunity to guide and teach them every day. We could instill in them our values, and the values of our community.

I tried to teach them to find enjoyment in their work, and to always see the funny side of life.

One day, in late summer, the kind of day when the sun casts a soft, slanted light, and you know the hectic, busy days of summer are winding down, I told the two girls to each grab a pail and a five-gallon bucket, we were going to pick chokecherries. They grumbled a little bit, but they did as I'd asked.

Jim and the boys were cutting grain in the back forty. They could park the grain trucks under the tall chokecherry trees, and we could stand on the top of the cabs and pick the big, ripe berries that we couldn't reach from the ground.

We had three or four five-gallon buckets, and we each had a smaller pail to pick into. When we had filled all of the large buckets, we left them in the trucks to be

dropped at the house later. We started the long walk home, carrying our pails to fill along the way.

We picked and picked, until I didn't think there was a single berry left on the place. Our pails were filled almost to the brim by the time we got back to the barn. Then I spied one little bush that had quite a few berries on it. "Let's get these to top things off." "Oh Mom," said the girls, "We're tired, and we have enough."

"Waste not, want not," I replied in my motherly way, as I reached into the bush for the berries. That's when I heard the angry buzz, and saw the hornet's nest, and the evil white face of a mad bald hornet.

The next thing I was aware of was being in the corn field, running as hard as I could go. When I finally came to my senses, I went back to see if the girls were okay. As I stepped out of the field, there was my empty pail lying about fifteen feet from where I had been standing when my mind was overcome by fear. My berries were scattered across the ground. I must have tossed that pail straight into the air.

My girls were also lying on the ground, convulsed and shrieking with laughter. "Oh Mom," they choked out, obviously enjoying my panicked reaction to what I had perceived as a great threat to my person. "We didn't know you could run so fast, or cuss like that." They sure were good at seeing the funny side of life! Lesson

number ???: I had stopped counting lessons by then, but I'm sure it was something like this: Don't be greedy, save something for the beasts of the fields.

I remember my father telling me over and over, when I was a child, that greed is a terrible sin, and that it will come back to bite you. You were right, Dad. I thought about that as I picked up my empty pail and walked to the house.

Kids have always played the major role in my life. Starting at the age of seven, I frequently found myself in charge of my younger brother and sister.

At different times, two of my nephews lived with us, and I loved them like they were my own. There has always been room in my heart and in my home for kids.

There were always extra kids on the ranch. They loved it there, and sometimes they'd stay for days before their parents would make them come home. I didn't mind; they brought joy and laughter into my life, and they knew they were always welcome.

With that many kids around all of the time, I had to have order, so that I could get my work done without a bunch of mishaps. I had my rules, and they all had to obey the rules.

After one boy grew up, he always liked to say, "Carol was always fair. When one kid got a cookie, we all got a cookie, and when one kid got a spanking, we all got a spanking." I loved that kid, and he called me Mom until the day he died.

Life wasn't all work. We had a lot of good times, too. There was skiing on Hitt Mountain. There all the 4-H projects, the hunting, fishing and camping.

Our kids were all involved in the various school activities. They played football and basketball. The girls were into cheerleading and gymnastics. Both of the boys played the trumpet all through high school and junior high. The girls took piano lessons, and they all took swimming lessons at the Midvale pool.

They had horses and bikes to ride with their friends. They had acres to play on, and creeks to swim in on a hot summer day. There was a skating rink and a movie theater in town while they were growing up.

Life on the ranch wasn't always easy. There was hard work, laughter, sometimes there were tears.

But there was always love, and through it all we were a family.

Happy Birthday, Mom!

In memory of Katherine Wilson, who would be

100 years old in April.

By Sandra Lund, Cambridge

When I was 14 years old I had no money for a Mother's Day gift, and it made me sad. I watched my mother sleeping on the couch, her white hair falling to the floor. I watched her, content that her breath was steady.

She'd been so tired that her gardening gloves were laying near her, not put away. I looked out the window into her garden. It was what she did in the summertime when school was not in session. In other seasons her garden consisted of children. Now, in this warmer season, she was easy to find among her plants.

She was all ours. I was her youngest, and so I had this view of an older mother whose essence could be caught in the beauty of one of her amazing flowers. To really see my mother, one would look into her classroom full of color, music and joy. To really see her, one would

look at her abundant garden of flowers hedging vegetables that seemed to sing, holy with color. What could I give this woman who was really a little sun that drew pretty things around her, all of them clambering for her attention so that she would know they'd learned what she'd taught them? Even the flowers outside watched her as she worked, hoping to be the very best example of her love. What could I give her?

I wrote her a poem.

"I Remember the Orange Rose" had one line I still remember: *I remember the orange rose and the poem I wrote that caught her.* Mom loved and treasured that poem, and somehow this exercise became a yearly event. Whenever her birthday or Mother's Day was looming I thought of the orange rose. After she passed, it became a way of honoring her once more.

Recently my brother-in- law said I should write my mother's story. He had helped her with her resume years before, and so he was aware of her education and of her work history. "You should write it," he said. "Her story would be a wonderful example to single mothers today."

He went on to remind me that after my father died, she updated her credentials and prepared herself to teach at the elementary school level after having taught

college students. She did that in order to keep us all together. Relatives were making plans to adopt one or two of us and find other homes for the rest. They said she could not support us on a teacher's salary. Well, not in Arkansas, she couldn't, she knew.

After her classes were complete, she gathered all six of us into our '56 Chevy and drove us to California.

Mothers are amazing. I've never known a truly loving mother not worthy of a medal of honor. The same goes for truly loving fathers. All the same, people are human. My mother was human. How do I write my mother's story while my siblings are still living to call me on details? I'm the youngest. I can wait, I thought. Meanwhile, there's always the Orange Rose legacy.

I'm writing Mom's story now, but that is only because of the Orange Rose. Rather, it is because of the latest edition of the poem (2018). It will explain something.

Mom seems to be on my mind more and more. I know she's passed, and I know that ghosts are probably only demons pretending to be a lost loved one. That's what I believe. But this is different. There is such a thing as "The Great Cloud of Witnesses." The Bible says so. I have felt my mother's love and joy several times since her passing. I've felt her forgiveness envelop me for all those times I fell short of her expectations and all those times I fell short of treating her as she deserved to be

treated while she was here. It's time I shared. And I want to begin with one of my best memories, that explained in 2017's Orange Rose.

Mom taught school in a small beach community about thirty minutes from our home, and she took me with her. That meant riding with her past sunrises and sunsets on the Pacific every school day. I do not remember a morning or an evening that she missed telling me to look deeply into the colors.

I Remember the Orange Rose

By Sandra Lund, Cambridge

2017

It seems strange to be honored in this way

When I think of my own Mamma today,

For as much as I did, as much as I tried,

I was not near the teacher, not near the guide.

When younger I scoffed at the things that she did,

Took offense at some of the things that she said,

But now, it's the orange rose I see

In the midst of her garden, planted for me.

It tells of the tireless love she spent,

And the smile only heaven could have sent.

It's the color of sunset kissing the sea,

A lone rose making a memory:

"You see," she would say as we passed the shore,

"That sea and that sunset are not just one more.

The color, the pattern are never the same."

And as I gazed at the setting once again:

She said I must look well, for I'd never see

Quite the same color as this one would be.

Oh, Mamma, I do. I remember it well,

Like an echo at sunset, I still hear you tell:

"It will never be quite this way again."

And now? Well, I long for one more "then."

I do not remember quite the last day

We passed by the ocean's shore.

They';ve blended into endless shades,

Maybe a million or more.

Now my hair is gray, as yours was then

But I still cannot remember when

Things exactly changed,

For always, it seems, the even's rose

Comes back to remind me again.

"Look!" you'd say, and "Treasure this!"

Till I'd finally looked up from my play.

You tended me well in your garden dear,

You pruned and watered and fussed.

When I'd complain, you'd say, "Look again!"

And then, "Why, God made you perfectly."

But, I know it was the love you spent,

The outrageous smile only God could have sent,

For the rose still blooms, and nightly shares

A new truth to say that God still cares.

My heart is now His as it once was yours,

For you called me to look at those many shores.

I remember the orange rose with love,

And my childhood eye still sees this truth

From my knees as He smiles from above:

He is ever new. And so, I remember

Forever the orange rose, and endeavor

With each color I paint into prose

To say, "Look! And look well,

You'll not again see this color,

Nor pattern like this one, just so."

This Mother's Day 2018
I Remember the Orange Rose

By Sandra Lund, Cambridge

A new rose grows in my heart today.

Although yearly it blossoms,

And yearly I write a rose poem to pray

Whose color is orange;

But this one is even more real and true.

This year its color

Looks much more like you.

"I remember the orange rose,"

I would always say

To honor you, Mother

On your special day…

Whose hair was once a silver-bright,

Washed by the thorn of a crimson rose

Until orange, and then finally white.

Past cares are no more, nor ever will be

Present in our memory,

For I see your green eyes twinkling now,

And the play of youth on your golden brow

While you wait on a shore I long to see,

In a cloud, as a witness,

Watching me.

You are holding a gorgeous white bouquet,

And your voice, in joy, compels me to pray.

Mother's Day, Age 94

By Bonnie Evans, Midvale

We walked her home from her church across the street with long stemmed roses in hand, yellow and rusty orange. Gorgeous. Someone really put out for those.

"We'll come back after lunch and help you with your flower gardening," we told her since we had just had a nice potluck meal the day before at a funeral dinner. She cried real tears at that one, even though the lady lived to be 100. But she was "sister" of 80 years. And we all sang Mom's favorite song, impromptu, "In the Garden." Perfect.

So back we went after Sunday lunch, taking her snap dragons and a bag of potting soil. We just had to do a little light gardening, ready the pots and get the snap dragons in them, do some light pruning, etc. But lo and behold, we found a large box on her carport with five big rose bushes nestled in wet newspaper, from Spring Hill.

"What?" I asked. "You told me you weren't buying any bushes, trees, etc. because you didn't know if you'd be here next year?"

She confessed, "But I couldn't pass up such a good deal!"

So Steve hauled out a shovel and started digging five deep holes. I found an old box of rose fertilizer in her cupboard and poured some in and filled the holes with water. Then she said, "They have to soak at least two hours in a bucket before they're planted, but no longer than twelve." Oh.

So we came home and watched the news and an old episode of Perry Mason, then back we went to get her investment into the ground.

The snapdragons? Well, she hadn't bought them for her containers after all. She wanted them in the ground along the end of her trailer. Down on the knees I went, digging, fertilizing, and praying the little ones would survive there in the hot sun.

Her contribution? I had thought she would like to get her hands in the dirt and had put her in a chair at a card table with the pots and soil. "No, I'd just like to watch you," she said.

OK. When I'm 94 I'll know what to do now.

Thanks, Mom
For My Inheritance

By Marie DeKnikker, Cambridge

Riches beyond measure,

Riches, for a lifetime, will I treasure.

Your desire to have me near,

Expresses your love, oh, so dear.

Sparkling eyes and smiling face,

Welcoming me with elegant grace,

No amount of money could replace,

The warmth of your dear embrace.

Recalling days of yesteryear,

Lessons learned, constantly reappear,

Laboriously, you generously gave your all,

Winter, Spring, Summer and Fall,

Nary a word of complaint, do I recall,

Exhibiting not one hint of pall.

Our trip to Hawaii, was the greatest of fun,

Protecting me on the beach, while in the sun,

And, accompanying me on the helicopter ride,

A guardian angel by my side,

Then, donning a hula skirt, you did abide,

Proof of our trip, never mind the chide.

Family Christmases and birthdays at your home,

Remembered by all, no matter where they roam.

An exemplary woman with humble heart,

Your precious non-monetary gifts depart,

 To your future generations, a generous start,

Hope I can do as well and be as smart.

Happy, blessed 93rd Birthday, Mom!

Thanks for your love and hugs, my riches, my inheritance!

My Teacher, My Waterbearer

By Cindy Loggins Hale, Midvale

You fed me – a hungry, thirsty soul

With nuggets of truth,

With great draughts of living water.

Patiently, for much was dropped or wasted.

You bore my numerous misadventures,

My pains of sorrow, my flickering faith,

And waited for the precious moment

When my soul was open, ready to hear:

Sufficiently nourished, in its many needs,

To listen.

Then, lovingly, you applied your energy

To helping me see, and more importantly,

To feel

The immense undergirding of Love,

That great Foundation

Upon which to build my own house of Faith.

You illustrated the importance of action

As building material;

Because a house of straw –

Of shallow purpose, of fleeting interest,

Is rarely shelter in the storm of life.

My walls begin to brick up nicely now;

I shelter and feed others as I can.

I see what you did, and oh, it is not easy.

I thank you.

A Memorial Tribute to Irna Collins

By Marie DeKnikker, Cambridge

Dear Momma,

You're Always On My Mind and especially while I'm _On the Road Again_, traveling with my electronic, musical companions, Elvis, George, Bobby and Willie. Their songs so aptly describe my feelings.

I'm wondering, _What's Going On In Your World_, for _I'm So Lonesome, I Could Cry_ and am! _I Loved You Because_ you were you. _It Isn't The Same Without You._

I left Cambridge, for Anderson, CA, on 5/6 to attend a wedding of one of my former first graders. Since it is a long trip, I stopped at Cedarville, our old stompin' ground, to visit and stay overnight with Diana, our former neighbor. On the morning of the seventh, I visited Anola and Clevon at Lake City. Remember them? Their health has faded since you last saw them. He barely weighs 100 lbs. Both are walking with canes, now. They remembered you and Dad with loving thoughts.

I ventured on to Gerber, where Cousin Karen and Mike live in their retirement home. They weren't home but generously offered to let me stay there to make for less traveling. I'd been there only once, but I did find their home and the hidden key! They had gone to San Jose, where she has her law practice and to attend a picnic and birthday party for a group of her clients and Mike! Their menagerie of livestock reminded me of you at the ranch. Tomorrow I shall try to find the location of the wedding, since I haven't found the place where I put the invitation for safe keeping.

In the meantime, my heart aches and I long for _Your Loving Arms_. I'll think about _Our Good Times_, although _It Keeps Right On A Hurtin'_.

There Were No Tomorrows for you after April 21, 2010. _The Grass Was Green and the Sky A Baby Blue_ when family and friends, with tears in their eyes, came to say their good-byes. I know how much _You Wanted To Go Home_ to the ranch to enjoy _The Green Grass of Home_, but instead Our Heavenly Father called you. I know He is taking good care of you, for His is a _Love Without End_.

Until we meet again, _I'm Without A Song_.

Love and hugs,

Your daughter Marie

Grandma's House

By Carol Cutler Bumgarner, Cambridge

I love to go to Grandma's house,
She does such funny things.
She washes dishes all by hand,
And as she works, she sings.

Grandma makes her meals from scratch,
I don't know what that means,
But we've been to the garden,
Where we picked squash, and beans.

I help my Grandma mix, and stir,
She sewed aprons so we'd match.
I don't understand it when she says,
The cookies are a batch.

Her bread comes from the oven,
Not from the grocery store.
And when the bread is all used up,
Then Grandma bakes some more.

She doesn't have a Swiffer,
She sweeps up with a broom,
And as she scrubs up with a mop,
She dances 'round the room.

We hang clean sheets out on a line,
Then put them on the bed.
It smells like sunshine and fresh air
When I lay down my head.

I say my prayers, and close my eyes,
And when I wake it's light.
Then when it's time for me to leave,
I hug my Grandma tight.

My Grandma doesn't have a lot
Of fancy stuff, and things,
But Grandma laughs, and plays with me,
And as she works, she sings.

My Mommy's Embrace

By Marie DeKnikker, Cambridge

Mommy, when you first held me and looked unto my face,

From that very moment I learned your sweet embrace,

I felt your gentle touch and smelled your fragrant skin,

You whispered that my life journey would now begin.

Stay near me through the years and watch me grow,

Teach me about life and love and all the things you know,

Before you realize it, time will pass and I'll be grown,

Teaching what you taught me to children of my own.

Embrace me now in your arms and

In your thoughts when we're apart,

For I know the special love shared within our hearts.

Love and hugs, Marie - March 31,2010

The Mustard Seed

From <u>Hang on Tight</u> by Sandra Lund, Cambridge

In honor of Katherine Wilson

My earliest memories house a picture of the one piece of jewelry my mother wore besides the gold band around her ring finger. It was a little glass ball encasing a mustard seed that hung from a gold chain around her neck. She never tired of telling me, "It is a mustard seed, and the Bible says that if you have faith the size of this tiny seed, you can move mountains."

This was not my first encounter with the concept of faith. In a family full of preachers and teachers, belief in God and the Bible was a given. Our grandmother was all about the Bible. She had her share of struggles in her lifetime, but when we knew her she was a rich man's widow and a preacher's wife. She lived in a charmed world of honeysuckle lanes and friends and cousins and church just next door, in a town with people she was either related to or had known all her life.

Mom was different. She was a determined mix of faith and struggles out of its disparities. This is perhaps part of the reason she had moved us all so far away from

her roots; she wanted us to find faith in its essence. In a very real sense, this is exactly what happened eventually. The faith we had would be sifted out of all our fears, a tiny mustard seed in a bucket full of sand that had turned hard – encasing it in glass like an idol until it took God himself to free the thing.

Life.

It seems that when I focused on my mother I saw life all at once. She was my sunshine and my shelter, my source of faith and the source of my biggest fear. Hindsight tells me that God gave me a picture of His love in her because her strength was His own; her weakness, His opportunity to gather fear together as a mirror to our absurd humanity and His amazing grace.

With Mom we were over a thousand miles from that comfortable Oklahoma Baptist anchor, our grandmother's world, and often it felt like we were, in fact, anchorless, lashed inside a sailboat with Mom at the helm in a raincoat and hat. As long as she was there, we were okay. When she threw up her hands in despair as she sometimes did in those early days after Daddy's death, we were not.

For me it was that same raincoat and hat I had nightmares about – the one Daddy wore the night he was killed. "Don't leave me!" I screamed. But he did.

He hugged me and handed me to my grandmother, then he kissed her and said goodbye at the door.

Would my mother leave me too?

For me this was a fear that went much deeper than what would I eat or where would I sleep. It was the fear of not knowing who would take the helm.

Life has a way of evening out. I once left my new trike behind Mom's Buick at night, and she ran over it by accident the next morning. I was determined to ride the thing, and somehow its brokenness fit my own exactly, so that the pride I had in being able to ride it was telling. I knew deep down I would not get a new trike, that I had to make do with two wheels, and so I did. When it came time for me to learn to ride my first two-wheeler, it was easier for me than it would have been otherwise. It was only the initial fear we had in common – me and the rest of the six-year-olds in the world. Somehow, I had something they did not. The grit I had developed turned into glass-hard determination around something that looked then about the size of a mustard seed.

As it turns out, Mom was right. When God came into my heart years later with His grace and shattered that hard glass shell that encased it, that seed could move mountains. And, if God could move my mountain, He could move others.

Who knew that when I grew up I would live in a world full of broken children who have never known their fathers – or worse – have been completely rejected by them? Who but God knew that when He broke that little seed out of its wall, I would never be fatherless again, and I would have a story to tell all those children – a story of hope. Who but God knew there would be a world of pain out there when I grew up – pain similar to the pain He had delivered me out of?

Who knew there would be so many in need of the story of someone who had witnessed the miracle of a determined little woman armed with a mustard seed and a trowel and the knowledge of the miracle that could happen when that seed was given up to God?

A Mother's Love

By Cindy Loggins Hale, Midvale

Music video available at https://tinyurl.com/ydbsosk7

A Mother's life is spent preventing harm,

Attention to all needs demanding

Yet in the shelter of her loving arms

Is my security.

A mother's heart encompasses her own

And also every child in need.

The seeds of motherhood and love are sown

In every kindly deed.

Chorus

A mother's love is always,

A granite wall, a tender, fragrant rose

Imperfect, beautiful and brave:

Thank God for the mother He chose.

A mother's strength is often said to be

A legend leading all her family

Yet, in her daily walk, a mother's led

To build a history.

A mother's soul inspires decency,

Beyond the grave her love lies surely.

When disappointments, trials and sorrows come,

The love she taught us glows.

Chorus:

A mother's love is always,

A granite wall, a tender, fragrant rose

Imperfect, beautiful and brave:

Thank God for the mother He chose.

The Little Lamb

By Heidi Hoskins, Cambridge

I was born on a cold winter day in early 2009. The first thing I remember was a bright light and cold. I remember strange sounds, smells and the warmth of my mom's wooly body. My twin was born a few minutes after me. He was dark, wet and small, while I am red, wet and big. Our mother immediately licked and cuddled us. She nuzzled us with her warm snout. I remember her wonderful scent and her loving purr-like sounds. My brother and I both cried until Mom soothed us with her gentle, warm nudges. How I loved Mom. I felt so safe and warm with her. I had this urgency like I needed to stand, but I didn't think I could. I tried several times but kept toppling down. Mom gently encouraged me. Finally, I did it! I was very wobbly and weak and barely able to stand. To make matters worse, something inside the middle of me was hurting. I didn't know what was wrong. I was still cold and shaking, but I felt the need to cuddle. As I was cuddling Mom's side and stomach I felt something warm and good I continued to suckle and the aching left my insides. I felt so much better!

Days passed and my brother and I both grew. How we loved to be near Mom while she grazed! We enjoyed

the warm sunshine and the smell of the sweet grass in the summer breeze. Sometimes my brother and I would run off a little way and play with the other new lambs. We would jump, twist and run. It was such fun! Then we would hear the familiar "baaaaaaah, baaaaah" and we would run quickly back to Mom's side. When we reached her, we would give her a gentle push with our heads under her belly while our little tails wagged with joy as we drank to our fill. In the meantime, Mom would always clean us. After we had our fill we would often lie down on the warm grass or dirt and curl up for a long nap near Mom. Brother and I would often curl up together as we enjoyed the sound of buzzing insects and the smell of the fresh, warm earth. Sometimes we would sleep near Mom in the barn, on the sweet-smelling fresh straw. Occasionally, during the night we would hear frightening sounds, such as dogs barking and coyotes yipping. Mom would snuggle closer to us to calm us.

As time passed we spent less and less time with Mom and more time with the other lambs playing chase. We also played a fun game called "butting," where we would run towards each other and crash heads together. Sometimes we would just pretend we were going to crash heads and other times we would really crash hard. Mom would still keep an eye on us as she grazed with the other sheep and made sure that we did

not wander too far. I really liked my home on Goodrich Road. We had lots of room to run and play and lots of good food.

One day some humans came that I had never seen before. They took me away to a new home on Cemetery Road. My brother stayed with Mom. I was very sad at first and missed my family. I cried "Maaaaaa, Maaaaaaa," because I missed the scent of my mom so much, however I soon made a lot of new friends and I began to like my new home and humans.

At my new home we lived on a hill so we could see far below and there were mountains above us. There were also several sheep. Some of the new sheep were boys and the humans called them rams. The boys kept following me around and at times I became annoyed. There was one boy in particular that had four large horns. He was very handsome and his name was Papa. I kind of liked him, but the others were not my type.

My new humans were very good to me and the woman liked to give me back and butt scratches, which I just loved. The woman gave me a name and called me "Sweetie." I liked to follow her around because she gave me special treats. I ate a lot of the special treats and one day I began to notice I was gaining weight. I was also very hungry and moody.

One day I was not feeling so good, so I laid down in the sheep shed in some nice, soft straw. My stomach ached with a strong and strange pain. I was so scared. As I was lying in the straw the rhythmic pain became worse. My human mom came out to check on me late at night with a lantern. Finally, the pain stopped and I saw a strange, wet, dark and wooly little thing on the ground wiggling beside me. The human seemed very pleased. At first, I was frightened and did not know what it was. Where did it come from? It was making strange sounds. I became curious and immediately sniffed it. It had a familiar scent so I licked and cleaned this little thing. I began to comfort it. I snuggled and cuddled it to calm it. Finally, it stopped crying. Then I noticed he was just like my brother. He was a boy! I began to talk to him in soothing, loving tones. Slowly this little lamb attempted to stand. I tried to encourage him with soft nudges. After he fell a few times he finally was able to stand, however he was very shaky and scared. He stood a few minutes and then he began to draw closer to me and cuddled me for warmth. I loved my little lamb. I would do anything to protect him, even to the death. He was mine!

One bright spring afternoon, while the golden Balsamroot was blooming across the rolling, green hills and as my new lamb was cuddling close to my side, faint memories came to mind. I don't know where

these thoughts came from, but they made me a little sad and happy at the same time. I remembered fleeting moments of my Mom cleaning and snuggling me on a warm summer morning. I remembered the smell of her wool, and her loving, soothing sounds. I remembered sleeping close to her and hearing her rhythmic breathing and heartbeat. How I missed my Mom, but I will treasure the loving memories forever.

Remembering
My Spiritual Mothers

By Jennifer Hickey Neider, Cambridge

This is a tribute to two women that I consider to be my spiritual mothers. I will forever be grateful to Corrie ten Boom and Lori Wilkins for the profound impact they had on my life because they were willing to share their knowledge of the Bible and its influence on their personal lives. Until I became an adult, I did not know that a practical application could be made of the teachings in scripture. And until then, I honestly did not know *what* the Bible said. Although I had good moral parents, I was not raised going to church. Because of Corrie and Lori's influence, I became what many people would call a religious fanatic. I had figured out that I could not make it through my life without the information contained in that ancient book, and so I became a regular church attender and a studier of the Bible. As a result, I have many times experienced God's power in my own life. I have even been the recipient of more than one miracle. I have these two ladies to thank for getting

me started in my walk of faith which began in my early twenties. Their influence was life changing.

Corrie and Lorie had a common thread in that they both escaped with their lives from the Nazis during World War II. I first became acquainted with Corrie ten Boom when someone gave me a copy of her book, _The Hiding Place_. It was the account of her family's life in Holland before and during Hitler's rise and occupation. The ten Booms were Christians and she and her family started hiding Jews in their home, which was also a watchmaker's shop. Much of the story is about the wisdom passed to her and her siblings from their godly father, Casper ten Boom. They all ended up in Hitler's dreaded concentration camps and Corrie was the only one who lived to tell about the experience. She and her sister Betsy used their knowledge of the Bible in very practical ways to survive the horrors they experienced there. They proclaimed that "there is no pit so deep that God is not deeper still."

The Hiding Place was the first book I read after high school, where reading assignments always seemed boring. I could not put Corrie's story down. I remember crying at times. The story had a powerful impact on me. I became keenly aware of the simple comforts of life that I had taken for granted. I started being really grateful for a hot shower at night and

smooth sheets to sleep on. I realized I had never gone to bed hungry and that in all my life I probably never would because I had been born in America. From _The Hiding Place_ I learned about forgiveness. I gained a new perspective on death when I read about Corrie's very personal experiences of losing numerous loved ones. My own parents were never able to offer me comfort or hope when a family member passed. How did Corrie know that it would be important to share these insights on such emotionally intense events as she told her story to John and Elizabeth Sherril, the couple who recorded it? Because of this I gained a new perspective on eternity.

Although I never met Corrie ten Boom in person, I have always said that when I get to heaven she is one of the first people I will look up so that I can personally thank her for sharing her story with me. I want her to know how greatly it impacted my life! Truly, she is one of my spiritual mothers.

My other spiritual mother was Lori Wilkins with whom I got to enjoy a real-life friendship, and fellowship. When my youngest son was only six weeks old, she invited me to a ladies' Bible study in her home. Thankfully, babysitting was provided or I probably would not have been able to attend. In spite of my mother-in-law's warning that when she was

growing up in South Dakota, a bunch of people decided to study the Bible and ended up in an insane asylum, I accepted Lori's invitation. This was to have a profound effect on the rest of my life.

Lori would have been in her early thirties then; her husband was the town veterinarian and she was his assistant. How she ended up in Cambridge, Idaho, I do not know. She had been born in Poland and fled from there when she was only five years old. She walked out with her parents to escape the Nazis. She told of her father selling his coat to buy milk for her younger sister. Lori spoke broken English, and I loved listening to her because of her accent. She had a natural beauty and was very interesting because she was forthright in whatever she said. You never knew what she was going to say ... it was refreshing. Lori was creative, an artist, and so she put that into her teaching and made it fascinating. This intrigued me so that I wanted to get in and learn what was inside that Bible. I began to attend these studies every Monday morning, and I loved it. I began to grow spiritually. I learned through my own reading and through Lori's classes that I could apply this information to my everyday life.

The Wilkins's lived in a house across the street from the Catholic Church in Cambridge. I will never forget several large links from a rusty chain being displayed

in a wall of cubbies in her living room the first time I visited her home. I learned from Lori that there is art in everything. Up until this time, I thought it was just some frilly thing you might buy at a home decorating party to be hung on the wall. She had another piece, an abstract painting in many shades of green. I can still see it. It hung on her bathroom behind the toilet, and on it she had written, "nausea and vomiting". She was the most creative person I have ever met. She was outspoken and funny. It seemed that she knew God personally. She brought her Bible studies to life as creatively as she did her home.

It was no secret that Lori hated housework. Who had time for dusting when there was so much to create? She walked out the scriptures in her daily life, and I will never forget the lesson she taught from the Old Testament to illustrate this. She told about Joshua and Caleb going out to spy on the Promised Land and coming back to report: *God is with us, let us go up at once and possess it! We are well able to overcome.* So, what Lori did was tell us that she was dragging her feet about vacuuming, and she quoted that scripture, saying to herself, "Let me go up at once and possess this vacuum cleaner. I am well able to overcome!" And she vacuumed.

Eventually Lori and her husband Gerald moved their veterinary practice to Emmett, Idaho where they spent

the remainder of their lives caring for animals and ministering through the American Sunday School Union whenever there was an opportunity. After their four children were grown, Lori was able to spend more time being creative. She ended up receiving royalties from the Singer Sewing company for designs she came up with using their embroidery attachments. The designs always included a scripture from the Bible.

One day when Lori and Gerald were returning from Orofino, Idaho where Gerald had performed a wedding, a pickup passed them and pulled back too soon, clipping their motorcycle. Lori suffered several broken bones and Gerald did not live. The nurses at the hospital were told not to tell her of her husband's death until her condition was more stable, but she asked and she was told. In response to this news Lori said, "Oh! I'm so jealous." Again, no one could have guessed this response, but it was so typical of Lori. Her connection to eternity and the things of God was always evident. Three years later, after a brief battle with cancer, Lori joined Gerald in eternity. I have heard that there are colors in heaven that we have not seen here on earth and I have imagined that Lori is now involved with the creation of even more new colors.

I can still feel her vivacious presence. I can see her long dark hair pulled into her usual upsweep and I can

hear her engaging accent as she painted a picture with words, making the Bible come alive to me. I am so thankful for her!

Thank you, Lori, for inviting me to your house every Monday morning to study that ancient book!

Note: *Remembering My Spiritual Mothers* is a segment of Jennifer Neider's life story which she is in the process of writing.

www.ingramcontent.com/pod-product-compliance
Lightning Source LLC
Chambersburg PA
CBHW052144220626
47052CB00005B/1183